STONER
COLORING BOOK

Copyright 2020 @ Focus Coloring Cave
All Rights Reserved.

All rights reserved. No part of this publications may be reproduced, distributed, or transmitted in any form or by any means, including photocopying, recording, other electronic, or mechanical methods.

For any inquiries or questions regarding our books, please contact us at : **focuscoloringcave@gmail.com**

ISBN: 9798706597825

www.ingramcontent.com/pod-product-compliance
Lightning Source LLC
Chambersburg PA
CBHW082005110225
21772CB00041B/505